Dilophosaurus

Written by Rupert Oliver
Illustrated by Andrew Howatt

Library of Congress Cataloging in Publication Data

Oliver, Rupert.
  Dilophosaurus.

  Summary: Follows a large crested flesh-eating dinosaur through his day as he searches for food and encounters an erupting volcano.
  1. Dilophosaurus—Juvenile literature.
[1. Dilophosaurus.   2. Dinosaurs] 1. Title.
QE862.S3O454   1985   567.9'7   85-19400
ISBN 0-86592-215-2

Rourke Enterprises, Inc.
Vero Beach, FL 32964

Dimorphodon

Brachiosaurus

Dilophosaurus

Lystrosaurus

Rutiodon

Dilophosaurus

Mamenchisaurus

Plateosaurus

Chasmosaurus

Protoceratops

Segisaurus pushed through the undergrowth. Somewhere she had heard a small animal moving. Taking care not to make too much noise, Segisaurus crept around a bush and saw her prey. A tiny furry mammal was chewing away at a large millipede. So intent was the mammal that it did not notice Segisaurus.

Segisaurus dashed forward, arms outstretched and jaws gaping. Then, the mammal saw Segisaurus, but it was too late. The dinosaur grabbed the small creature and plunged her teeth deep into the warm flesh. As soon as Segisaurus started her meal she was disturbed by a tremendous noise. A massive foot came down and struck the ground right next to Segisaurus.

The great foot belonged to Dilophosaurus.
Dilophosaurus was hungry. He had not eaten
anything for several days. Luckily for Segisaurus,
Dilophosaurus was not interested in small animals.
He needed prey more suited to his size. Segisaurus
scampered off into the undergrowth. At that moment
the earth moved beneath Dilophosaurus' feet. For a
few seconds the ground swayed and Dilophosaurus
almost lost his balance. Then, everything was still.
Dilophosaurus was puzzled.

Dilophosaurus was now very hungry and as the ground was no longer swaying, he moved down to the beach to see if there was anything to eat. When he emerged on to the seashore he saw something which interested him.

Not far away was a Plesiosaur which had come ashore to lay her eggs. Dilophosaurus knew that Plesiosaurs could only move slowly and that they tasted delicious. Dilophosaurus chased after the Plesiosaur. In fear, Plesiosaur dragged herself along on her flippers in the hope of reaching the ocean. Just as she got to the surf, Dilophosaurus caught up with her. As the surf splashed around them, the two reptiles grappled with each other. Dilophosaurus tried to get his teeth around the vulnerable neck of Plesiosaur while the sea reptile attempted desperately to get away into deeper water where she would be safe.

After a while Dilophosaurus was successful in sinking his teeth into the neck of the Plesiosaur and the surf became stained red with the blood of the dying reptile.

Dilophosaurus dragged his kill up the beach, away from the waves. Once again the ground suddenly shook. Dilophosaurus looked around in alarm, but he could not see anything of which to be frightened. He did not notice the smoke coming from an island out to sea.

A loud roar startled Dilophosaurus. Emerging from the trees was another Dilophosaurus. He smelled the fresh meat of the Plesiosaur and he was very hungry. The new arrival advanced on Dilophosaurus roaring loudly and displaying his crests in an attempt to frighten Dilophosaurus. Dilophosaurus stood his ground and shook his crests at the other dinosaur. Then, a female Dilophosaurus appeared from the trees and joined her mate in frightening Dilophosaurus. Dilophosaurus realized he was no match for two dinosaurs so he took a last bite of meat and backed away.

Dilophosaurus was very disappointed. He had lost his kill and was still very hungry. Now, he would have to find some other food. There was no other creature along the beach, for the roaring of the dinosaurs had frightened everything away.

Dilophosaurus climbed up the steep hill behind the beach to look for food further inland. Then, the earth shuddered one more time. This was immediately followed by a tremendous explosion and the island off the coast disappeared in a sheet of flame. A cloud of smoke shot up from the island high into the air.

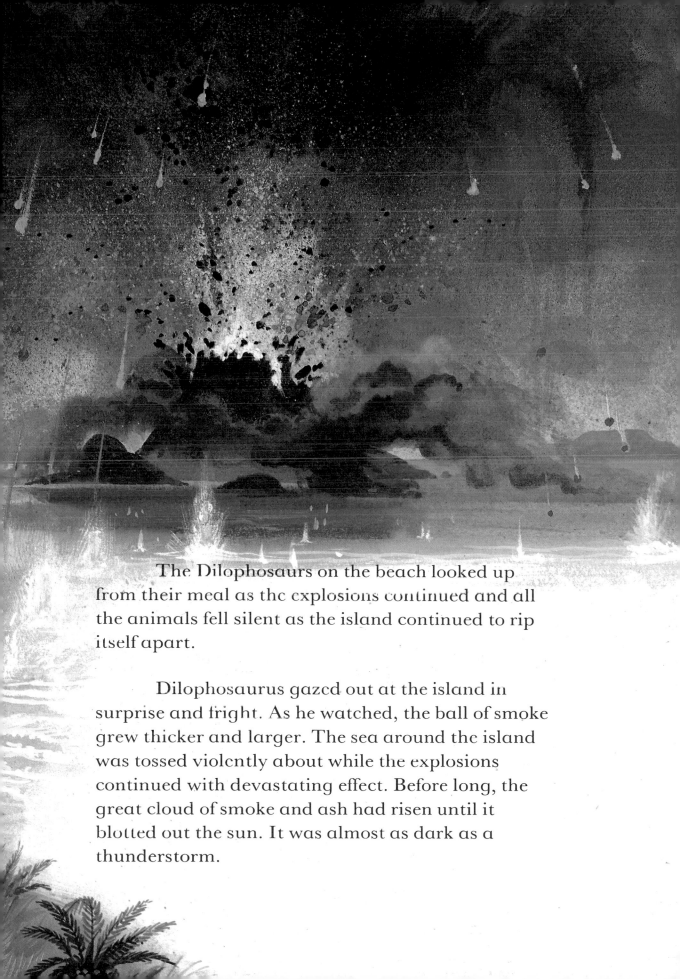

The Dilophosaurs on the beach looked up from their meal as the explosions continued and all the animals fell silent as the island continued to rip itself apart.

Dilophosaurus gazed out at the island in surprise and fright. As he watched, the ball of smoke grew thicker and larger. The sea around the island was tossed violently about while the explosions continued with devastating effect. Before long, the great cloud of smoke and ash had risen until it blotted out the sun. It was almost as dark as a thunderstorm.

Then, a sudden whooshing noise startled Dilophosaurus from his grazing. He looked around and saw a huge boulder fall from the sky. Again, the noise like a tremendous wind came and another rock smashed into the ground. Dilophosaurus was very confused. Nothing like this had ever happened before and he was frightened.

Rocks were falling all around him now. Dilophosaurus moved toward the trees, perhaps they would give him some shelter from the falling rocks. Then, one of the rocks plummeted down and crashed into Dilophosaurus. Dilophosaurus gave a roar of pain and fell to the ground. His leg was hurting and he could not get up.

As Dilophosaurus lay on the ground nursing his wound, a new and strange sound came to his ears. It was like the booming of distant thunder and it was coming from out of the sea. Dilophosaurus looked down to the beach. The other two Dilophosaurs were still eating the Plesiosaur, but something had changed. The water was running out to sea, leaving a broad stretch of sand.

The booming grew louder and Dilophosaurus looked in alarm as a wall of water, many feet high rushed shoreward from the ocean. The enormous wave swept aside the two Dilophosaurs on the beach and they disappeared beneath the water. Then, it smashed into the hill where Dilophosaurus was resting. Water splashed everywhere and even Dilophosaurus was drenched.

When the massive wave had subsided the beach was left empty. There were no Dilophosaurs and no Plesiosaur. The island continued to belch smoke, but the explosions had stopped.

Dilophosaurus tried to stand up. His leg was very painful where it had been hit by the rock. Eventually, he got to his feet and hobbled off to look for food. Dilophosaurus had been hurt, but he would soon be better.

Dilophosaurus and Early Jurassic Arizona

The Day of the Dilophosaurus

The history of the world is very long and very complicated. Scientists only know about much of it by digging in the rocks and finding fossils. By looking at the rocks in which fossils occur, scientists can tell how old the fossil is. To help them do this scientists have divided the entire history of the world into eras and each era is further divided into periods. The dinosaurs lived during the Mesozoic Era which began about 225 million years ago and ended about 65 million years ago. The Mesozoic Era has been divided into three periods: the Triassic, the Jurassic and the Cretaceous. The fossils of Dilophosaurus have been found in rocks dating from the early part of the Jurassic period. This means that Dilophosaurus lived about 190 million years ago.

Arizona of long ago

The very first Dilophosaurus fossil to be discovered was found by a Navajo Indian in Arizona in 1954. From these remains scientists have been able to reconstruct the appearance and way of life of the dinosaur. Other fossils which have been found dating from the same

time as Dilophosaurus have shown us the kind of world in which it lived. We know for instance that the area now known as Arizona was very different from the near-desert landscape to be seen today. The vegetation was rich and varied, and it was this which allowed the wide variety of animals to survive. Some of the plants would appear familiar to us today. There were conifers and monkey puzzle trees, as well as dozens of different types of ferns. Other plants, however, such as the cycadeoids and tree ferns have long been extinct and appear strange to our eyes. At the time, North and South America were not connected. They separated from each other a few million years before our story takes place.

Lifestyle of Dilophosaurus

Dilophosaurus was a large meat-eating dinosaur. It was about twenty feet long, which made it one of the largest animals alive at that time. Its powerful build and sharp teeth were ideal equipment for attacking other animals

Megalosaurus, a much larger relative of Dilophosaurus which lived in Europe.

Jurassic plants which are now extinct

tree fern

cycadcoid

and for eating meat. It belonged to a family of dinosaurs known today as the Megalosaurids, which means "great lizards". Megalosaurids were one of the most successful groups of dinosaurs. They lived over a period of many millions of years and evolved into numerous species. Dilophosaurus was different from other Megalosaurids because of the pair of bony crests on its head. These crests have puzzled scientists ever since the Navajo Indian first found fossils of this dinosaur. They are paper thin in places and would have been far too thin and fragile to stand up to rough treatment. It is possible that only males had these crests and that they were used as a type of display. In our story, Dilophosaurus uses them in this way when he tries to frighten the other Dilophosaurs away from his food.

Animals of the time

The animal life of the Early Jurassic was just settling down after a period of immense change. The dinosaurs had evolved a few million years earlier and had pushed most other forms of land reptiles into extinction. Segisaurus was an early member of the dinosaur family known as

Coelurosaurs. These small nimble hunters survived until the end of the Mesozoic. Ammosaurus was one of the last prosauropod dinosaurs. These creatures died out to give way to the Sauropods which were beginning to appear. Scutellosaurus was the last dinosaur to be found in early Jurassic Arizona. It was one of the earliest members of the Ornithischians, a large group of dinosaurs which became very successful millions of years after Dilophosaurus died out.

There were many other animals alive at the time, apart from dinosaurs. Many species of insect flew through the air, as did rather primitive Pterosaurs, the flying reptiles. Mammals could be found scurrying around in the undergrowth. One of these small mammals can be seen as a prey of Segisaurus in our story. Mammals remained small throughout the Mesozoic but later became the dominant form of land life and gave rise to man. In the sea lived several types of reptiles including the Plesiosaur which Dilophosaurus kills in the story and some species of Ichthyosaur. Ichthyosaurs were reptiles which looked like modern dolphins and were very successful.